Poems of Love
for
Jesus and for You

by

Natalia Beller

© 2017 Natalia Beller / Autorin

1. Auflage
Umschlaggestaltung, Illustration: Natalia Beller
Verlag: tredition GmbH, Hamburg

ISBN 978-3-7439-4217-2 (Paperback)
ISBN 978-3-7439-4218-9 (Hardcover)
ISBN 978-3-7439-4219-6 (e-Book)

Bibliografische Informationen der Deutschen Nationalbibliothek:
Die Deutsche Nationalbibliothek verzeichnet diese Publikation in der Deutschen Nationalbibliografie; detaillierte bibliografische Daten sind im Internet über http://dnb.b-nb.de abrufbar.

Thank you

Jesus Christ, my God, my Lord, my Savior,

you saved me. My life has changed the moment I came to know you. Nothing will ever be the same and no one and nothing can compare to you and to what you've done for me. I look forward to every journey, I look forward to every plan you have for me, and I look forward to every day. Not one experience have I lived through without you. You are always with me. I love you with all my heart and all my soul.

Mom, Dad & Anna,

my family. You are the people who love me and are there for me no matter what. I was placed with you by God for a reason. Your love is astounding and never-ending. I wouldn't be where I am without your support. Thank you for loving me.

Isabella & Simone,

the angels in my life disguised as my best friends. Without you I wouldn't have survived the heartaches, the pain, the challenges. You share with me my happiest moments and you comfort me when I'm down. You accept and love me for who I am and I never have to hide anything from you. It's been years now and more decades will pass and I only want to spend them with you.

Marc M., Jennifer D. A., Michael P., Markus G., Malwina P., Madeleine U., Josip G. K., Hans S., Todd F., Erika J. & Julia W.,

thank you for your friendship, guidance, inspiration and comfort. You will always have a special place in my heart. I will never forget the things you have done for me.

Last but not least, YOU,

thank you for reading this. I poured out my most inner feelings to show you that whatever you go through, you are not alone. We all face challenges and obstacles and we all share this big rock called earth. I hope my words will help you, maybe guide you, hopefully encourage you and show you the greatness of God's love. Trust in him, because he knows how to protect his children. Much Love and may the Lord always bless you.

Contents

New Life

There was once a girl that was so lost
Although she thought she had it all
Some days she cried herself to sleep
Couldn't take the loneliness no more
There was a girl she felt oppressed
Like she was dying in the cold
And like there's nothing in her life
That could give shelter from the storm

She's been hurt a million times
By the ones she loved the most
The worst part was she never even
Did anything to them in return
She felt like she was being punished
For something she had never done
And she desperately tried to understand
Why she had to bear it all

No one would remember her birthday
When they were in need she would help
No one would ask her how she felt
But when they cry she's always there
No one would ask if she needed something
But when they were helpless she didn't hesitate
And when the time came she was in need
She found herself lonely and desolate

This world's unfair, this world's so cruel
Why are people rude and self-involved?
They never even seem to have a clue
How much damage they all cause

A word is not just a simple word
There's power in every one
A word can heal you and give you hope
Or destroy you for the nonce

She never knew what kind of love
Could exist in this cold world
Before God came so full of peace
And gave her a reason to hold on
She saw herself in his glowing eyes
His abundant love for her
She saw the reason he gave her life
God's plan revealed to her

With his power so great and holy
He made decades of pain go away
Everything she faced now made sense
Every tear she cried felt undone again
Within a tiny little second
The Lord, her savior, showed her true love
And it stayed with her until this day
And won't leave her abandoned nor alone

Exhausted

I'm exhausted, I'm so tired
I am so sick, I am blear-eyed
Unmotivated, I'm uninspired
I am drowning, like I'm dying

I'm exhausted, I give up
I am straining, out of luck
I'm so confused, like I'm stuck
I'm aggressive, I'm so fed up

I'm exhausted, I hate this world
I'm isolated and so alone
Inconsolable, no one's there
Always crying, no one cares

I'm exhausted, two faced liars
They're hypocrites, pricey attire
Broken heart, too much to bear
Defeated soul, trying to mend

I'm exhausted, where's the help?
I am so lost, destroyed myself
Reaching out for saving grace
But I'm exhausted, longing for death

Dreaming

You give me the desires of my heart
Before I even know them
It's hard to understand your ways
But your ways are always perfect
The nights still have me wondering
Why do we have dreams?
Not the ones we simply wake from
But the ones that stick with us through everything
The kind of dreams we see with open eyes
Cause we carry them inside our hearts
Why do these kinds of dreams exist?
They sometimes tear us apart
Unfulfilled desires
Will make you doubt yourself
Satan whispering in your ear
You're unwanted and worthless
Don't listen to the gloomy voices
Ignore the darkness in your head
It's a poisonous state of mind
Distracting you from true fate
So keep on dreaming
With your eyes facing the Lord
His hand will guide you
He'll always hold you close
His ways and plans for you are perfect
You shall prosper in everything you do
He will steer all circumstances
And make all things work out for you
Do not search for earthly pleasures
Your reward will be with our God
Give all your burdens to him
You don't have to face your challenges alone

© N. B. 03 / 2016

Enough

Stay with me, just a little bit
Please don't leave me, I'm so alone
Hold my hand and hold me close
Dry my tears cause I need your love
Just a little while will be enough
Will be enough

You're the one that I want close
You're the one that I trust most
With you I won't end up all hurt
With you I know I'm finally home
Just a little while will be enough
Will be enough

And I don't care about tomorrow
With you I forget all of my sorrows
Stay right here and I'll promise you
I'll make you feel the same way, too

Just a little while will be enough
Will be enough
Just a little while will be enough
Will be enough

You don't know what you're giving me
With just one word or when you look at me
I love your smile, I love everything
Not one inch on you I don't cherish

Just a little while will be enough, will be enough
Just a little while will be enough, will be enough

© N. B. 01 / 2011

God's Plan

I remember when I was younger
No clue of the world and what was going on
No one talked about the meaning of life
I never heard anyone talk about God
God to me was just a word
With no meaning behind it at all
Something people thought existed
But he never seemed to be real

What does God want?
Who is God really?
Is he great, big and disastrous?
Does he love or is he mean?

Who is God really?

Kind of afraid of this "God"
But kind of curious
Didn't want to get involved
Drowned in confusion and kind of lost
Every night I would remember
The vision I had when I was seven years old
It was night time and out the window
I saw a man hanging and bleeding on a cross

Until much later I never heard of Jesus
No one even told me how he died
No one told me he died for all of us
Trying to keep his stories out of my life
I never heard of salvation
I never heard of giving my burdens to him
I never heard of prayer
I was 26 years old the first time I prayed

Three years later I realized
How the words of the Bible are true
In the last days the world will decline
And people will be selfish and cruel
It makes me so sad to realize
Only a few truly know God
And I could have gotten to know him 26 years ago

So I pray for everyone that I meet
That God's embrace will fall upon them
So that they live their life in peace
And be saved from hell
I never knew God doesn't want much
Love thy neighbor as you love yourself
All he wants is all of your heart
And for you to keep his commandments

God has something great in mind for you
Don't be afraid
God is with you

© N. B. 02 / 2016

Jesus Christ

I can't thank you enough for what you did
Not just for me but for everyone
But right now I just want to take this right here
And speak of everything you've done
Cause I want to thank you
I want to deeply thank you
For every single thing you did for me

You have taken me in when I was abandoned
You have listened when no one else did
You came to me when I was all alone
You healed my wounds and stopped the bleeding

You have chosen me when I rejected you
You pointed to me when I didn't look your way
You didn't give up on me even when I did
You gave me a purpose and reason to live

You dried my tears when I was crying
You heard my screams when I was in pain
You washed away every wrong thing that I did
You brought peace when I was in rage

You forgave the sins that I've committed
You washed away my awful past
You have come here not to judge me
But to show me your grace and your love

You don't stop blessing me
You give me everything that I want
You show me the things I truly need
And guide me through all storms

I can walk through any desperation
Despite all pain I will never drown
Because there's hope, there is salvation
There is redemption in your arms

We're not saved by being perfect
No one walking this earth can ever be
We're saved by your grace and your offer
Your sacrifice that overcame the enemy

And I want to thank you for this
I want to thank you indeed
For everything you've done for us
For everything you've ever done for me

A Drop Into The Ocean

If I give you my hand will you guide the way?
Will you try to understand what I'm trying to say?
If we walk for miles under thundering skies
Will you dry the tears that fall from my eyes?

Above us there's heaven, well I know it is
Down here we're wandering with our bitter tears
The stars shining brightly and the moon's risen high
But down here we're all blinded by dazzling lights

And like a drop into the ocean our tears will fall
No one's there to help us; we're all alone
Like a drop into the ocean no one hears our screams
We're standing here without hope
Facing the apocalypse

If I touch you I fear you're going to break
When I'm talking to you, you just look away
When I try to explain it, you don't care for my pain
And when I'm falling behind I know you won't wait

Do you see that around us, there's death and violence?
Do you feel that inside us there's nothing but hate?
The stars shining brightly and the moon's risen high
But down here we're all blinded by dazzling lights

And like a drop into the ocean our tears will fall
No one's there to help us; we're all alone
Like a drop into the ocean no one hears our screams
We're standing here without hope
Facing the apocalypse

Behind your mask I see your fears
I can feel you're very close to tears
You gave up like I did but you're still standing here
While the angels have left us with nothing but this
A legacy of agony

And like a drop into the ocean our tears will fall
No one's there to help us; we're all alone
Like a drop into the ocean no one hears our screams
We're standing here without hope
Facing the apocalypse

© N. B. 03 / 2011

Erika

I listened to this sermon
Wasn't moved by it at all
That day felt like it was numbing me from within
I felt some glances on me
Didn't care for them at all
The words felt like they weren't meant for me

But then she came
And this is what she had to say:

"The Lord wants me to tell you
You no longer have to be strong
Rest your hopes and all your dreams
On him when you're walking through the storm
It hurts him to see you suffer
He saw you crying every single time
He showed me what you've been through
And what has happened in your life
The Lord wants you to give him
All your struggles and your pain
You don't have to bear it alone
Give to him what you can't take
Why do you think your problems
Matter less than the ones of everyone else
Don't you know he loves you more than
You could ever understand
You pray for many people
God wants you to pray for yourself, too
You're so selfless and so modest
But God wants to fulfill your wishes, too
It's like he's standing right beside you
With tears running down his cheeks

Reaching out his hand for you
Waiting for you to finally turn to him
He's screaming out your name
He has such great plans for you
Don't rely on peoples' validation
But on the Father and trust his plans for you

The Lord wants me to tell you
He's been waiting for so long
When he formed you in your mother's womb
He knew how you'd come out
He was proud the day you were born
Heaven had a feast the day you accepted him
The Lord wants you to follow
And he completely wants to take you in
The Lord wants me to tell you
Your pain is now over finally"

Then I left the sermon
With a smile on my face
It was as if the pain has left my heart
I thought about the message
I thought about my fate
Looked up to the heavens right into his grace

© N. B. 02 / 2016

Drowning

Words can either mend you or tear you apart
They can either heal you or break your heart
Words have such great power of which you're not aware
They can fully destroy you or strengthen your faith

Guard your heart it's your inner source
It will decide what you do and say
Don't let it go and drown in darkness
The enemy comes to kill, steal and destroy

Words can either help you or push you down the stairs
They can either uplift you or let you drown in despair
Words were made to create
So watch out what you say out loud
Words can also devastate
And make you feel hated and alone

Don't be a hater, be a congratulator
Live up to what he created you for
Words have the power to give life
So go and give it instead of killing hope

Guard your heart it's your inner source
It will decide what you do and say
Don't let it go and drown in darkness
The enemy comes to kill, steal and destroy

© N. B. 02 / 2016

Lord, I'm Sorry For What You Witness

Whenever I take one look at the world
I quickly have to look away
And I want to stand before you my Lord
And apologize for everyone who's gone astray
I feel this aching inside my heart
Whenever they misinterpret what you've said
Because they teach that light is darkness
And the darkness is what saves

Whenever I hear this New Age stuff
I want to scream out in pain
How can people truly believe?
That they're godlike and can save themselves?

Why is their heart so far away from yours?
Why don't they try to find the truth?
Why do people believe in lies?
Instead of seeking you

When I see how they kill each other
I want to run so far away
You never taught us to kill anyone
You taught us to love in your ways
You died for us so we can live
You defeated the enemy
When I hear someone denying that
I want to scream out in agony

When I hear people badmouthing you
I want to burst out into tears
Still you won't give up on us
Until the ending of all days
Whenever I hear those hateful words
I can't help but feeling sad
Why did the world become so cruel?
You were here teaching us to love

My Lord, I'm sorry for what you witness
That your children live with hate
I want to thank you for your sacrifice
Every day you shower us with grace

You said to us, the truth will make you free
And I pray for everyone to find your truth
I want everyone to overcome the enemy
And not be tempted to turn their backs on you

They think that they don't need you
But without our Father we can't do anything
Fact is we are nothing without you

And I pray
Someday
Everyone will see

© N. B. 02 / 2016

Testimony

I was with him for three years
When God decided to call my name
I was confused and crying tears
Cause I didn't know what to do that day
I came to know God
I learned his ways
I was stunned by his abundant love
I wanted to share God
And his amazing Grace
I wanted him to know about this love

But then he said
He was sick of it
He didn't want
To hear a word of it
Why was he so mad?
I still don't understand?
So he made me choose
Between him and the God of Abraham

"It's either me or Jesus
Make your decision now
Either you stop this madness
Or you can pack your bags and go
I cannot accept your behavior
And the words that you speak
It's either me or Jesus
Now tell me, which one is it?"

I couldn't believe
The words that I heard
Why would he disclaim?
The truth of God's Word

So I looked up to the heavens
My eyes towards the sky
Listened to what my heart told me
I waited for a sign

Then I looked back at him
With a smile on my face
"Well then I will choose Jesus"
And I walked away

© N. B. 07 / 2017

Empty Me

Lord, I'm begging you
Empty me of me
Empty me of all the selfishness
And bitterness I carry
I'm asking you to empty me
Of all the hurt and all the pain
Lord, empty me of everything
That you never meant for me to have

Lord, I'm begging you
Empty me of me
Empty me of all the hate I feel
Help me forgive the ones that hurt me
I want for you to empty me
Of everything that's not pure and true
Empty me of my false self
So I can be filled with you

Lord, I'm begging you
Empty me of me
Empty me of all partiality
For people that have wronged me

I wish for you to empty me
Of everything I've ever done wrong
Empty me of everything unholy
Have my sins washed away by blood

Lord, I'm begging you
Empty me of this world
Empty me of every earthly pleasure
I wrongly ran after
Empty me of my ways
So that I can be filled with yours
Empty me of all mistakes
So that I can do your will and move on

Lord, give me a new heart
Renew my mind
Give me a new purpose
The one you chose for my life
Empty me of wrong thoughts
Wrong desires and all the lies
Empty me of me
So that in your name I may rise

Don't Worry About Me

I am strong enough to get through it
I know how to handle this situation
Don't waste your time to worry about me
It's not the first time of desperation

This is between me, myself and I
Only God knows about the details
For I know he is comfort, won't laugh in my face
He's the only one I let see under the surface

Cause the Lord doesn't need words
He sees my heart and knows what I think
Before I would even say it out loud
He knows exactly what I feel

So don't worry about me
There is nothing you can do
I appreciate your concern
But there is nothing you can do

God is the one and only
To make things work out for my good
So, don't you worry about me
God will guide me through

© N. B. 03 / 2016

I Hope This Is the Last Time

Oh Lord, please help me
I don't know how to handle these feelings
I don't know what's happening
What is happening to me?

Lord, I can't cope with this madness
How could my heart be so careless?
What am I supposed to do with this?
I can't seriously be falling for him

Is this a joke?
Did you do this Lord?
Why, after all this time?
Oh Lord, answer me, why?

I'm a grown up
This is not supposed to happen
I'm all grown up
How could I let this happen?

Lord take away these feelings
They're driving me insane

Erase these emotions
Cleanse my heart from anything
That drives me into madness

Because I'm going crazy
I'm going insane
I can't seem to shake the thoughts
Of him out of my brain

I fear I'm losing my mind
I fear I'm falling deeper
How can I get out of this?
I'm crying, losing sleep

Because there is another
He has a lover
There is another
And I won't be able to compete

How am I supposed to get through this?

Lord help me
Please help me

Please

© N. B. 06 / 2017

Alone

Every day seems to be exactly the same
No ups and no downs
No one's there that seems to care
It seems like time just stopped
It's becoming spring again
The cold months of winter are gone
Remains of cold rain on the window pane
And I'm feeling so alone

I wonder where the years went by
So many days but so few memories
It seems I let so much pass me by
Without taking ever seizing anything

And so, this is my result
A big pile of nothing
Not much to be proud of
I hope God will forgive me
I feel like I let him down
He wasted a whole life on me
I don't know how to make it better
I feel so undeserving

Lord, I'm sorry I'm disappointing
I don't know what you want

Father God, please forgive me
I don't understand your plans at all

The fire you set in my soul
Is still burning for you every day
But right now I feel that I lost control
And I can't find the words to explain
It feels like a heavy load on my heart
That impedes every step that I take
I dream about what could be
When at night I lay awake

And so this is my result
A big pile of nothing
Not much to be proud of
I hope God will forgive me
I feel like I let him down
He wasted a whole life on me
I don't know how to make it better
I feel so undeserving

Lord, I'm sorry I'm disappointing
I don't know what you want

Father God, please, oh please forgive me
I don't understand your plans at all

I Want To Fall In Love

They say the best memories contain love
And everything they're made of
Will accompany us for the rest of our lives
I once heard the best thing in this world
Is when your loved unconditionally
And someone takes a bullet for you anytime

But I'm wondering when
When
When
Will this time come for me?

When will it be my turn to find something just like this?

I had dreams about what they're all saying
I woke up sweating and with this aching
I forgot how scary this thing could truly be
If you're lucky enough you will be spared
Of all the heartache and disappointment
But isn't this what makes it all so great?

Cause I'm wondering how
How
How
Do they act like it's no big deal?

How come they all have something I can't receive?

I, too want to have this special feeling
I want to have someone who's there for me
I, too want to have this special feeling
I, too dream of having the same things

I want to fall in love
Cause I heard it's the best thing in the world

I have thoughts I tell no one
Hide the longing behind my walls
Hope my laughter covers up the scars
But I want to fall in love

I have secrets no one knows
This yearning inside that screams out loud
I'm so scared but I want to disallow
That I really want to fall in love

© N. B. 07 / 2015

I Love You

Crimson tears keep falling
I stopped counting
I've lost control
And you're blaming me for this
I know
You don't have to say anything
Cause I know what you think
And when I'm with you I can't breathe
Why is it like this?

You feel neglected
You feel misplaced
I stumble upon the piles of sorrow that you laid
I can read your mind
I know what you hide
But everything here remains the same

Cause I'll give you my blood
I'll give you my heart
I'll give you everything I am
We're running around in circles
And you pressure me again
But those words I could never say
You're sublime like I'm beneath you
You know I'd give you anything you want
But this time I fear I've lost you
You're impatient; it's been way too long
But this I can't say
I don't know how to say it
And you no longer want to wait

© N. B. 09 / 2009

Crescent

I remember those velvet skies
Where your words were my freedom
And being with you was my home
I can't help but sink into your eyes
Let myself get caught up in you again
And be reborn in your embrace

You're my saving grace
The moment I forget everything else
The softest touch, the sweetest kiss
And I'm never afraid

You're the angel watching over me
Guarding my dreadful sleep
Turning nightmares into pleasant dreams
Standing by my side

There's no darkness, night's aflame
Burning my fears like arid leaves
And insanity becomes rationality again

I find my inner silenced peace
In abstraction of every dreadful fear
And the nights become quiet again

You are my answer
To everything I've ever wished for
The instant when morning descends

Fasten me to your side
I lost it to this cold night
When I feel your breath on my skin
Bearing your smell in mind

Sweet hope arises
Cruel romance blowing in the wind
The dream I had lives in this scenery
Knowing that you'll always be with me

You're my saving grace
The moment I forget everything else
The softest touch, the sweetest kiss
And I'm never afraid

You're the angel watching over me
Guarding my dreadful sleep
Turning nightmares into pleasant dreams
Standing by my side

He Said

It's been days since I last heard from him
But his words keep ringing in my ears
It's been weeks since I last saw him
But his eyes keep hunting all my dreams

Again it ended like every time before
Can't believe how foolish I have been
Again I ended up getting hurt
And hating myself for letting him in

This time I thought he was heaven sent
He said all the right things
Too bad I never even realized
He would never really act on it

I can't understand what I've been feeling
I can't recall what made me trust in him
I wish I could turn back the hands of time
And save myself from this anguish

A million questions keep me up at night
Too many for me to sort out
Going through everything in my mind
What did I do to scare him off?

I never even knew
Someone could ever be this cold
To him those words were nothing sacred
But to me they meant the world

He said
But then he didn't
He said he would
But he never wanted
He told me lies
And I believed him
He said so much
Just to deceive me

And I believed everything

First Kiss

I know it was God's Grace
That brought me to this place
It was God's will
For me to ever get this far

I can't do anything without my Father
I can't even define what's right or wrong
He is my rock and my salvation
I put my life in his hands many years ago

And for everything I do in life
I trust him blind
I know his ways are perfect
In his name, I shall rise
For everything I say
It shall be said with love
Because he was the one to first love us
He gives all that I dream of

And now I dream of this
Something I never had before
I dream of true love's first kiss
Every lie shall then be gone
I dream of true love's revelation
A keeper of my heart
Someone that will guard it with his life
So that it will never break apart

Every night I dream of this
Something so pure and true
Of someone to appreciate me
Of strong arms, I can fall into
Someone to turn to after a rough day
Someone to lighten up my nights
I dream of someone to hold me
And go with me through every journey in this life

I want someone that's not scared
Of anything that might come
Someone bold enough to stand firm
Through temptations and all storms
Someone not afraid of true love
Of showing openly he cares for me
I want to find that someone
I can grow old with finally

And now I dream of this
Something I never had before
I dream of true love's first kiss
Every hurt shall then be gone

I Never Get What I Want

You said if I knock you will open
But I'm still standing outside
You said if I ask I'll be given
But my dreams have all died
You said you have plans for me
But I'm still all alone
You said if I take refuge in you
I'll be safe from all storms

But how come I feel so low?
How come I feel this pain?
How come I feel all this sadness?
How come I live my life in vain?

I never get what I truly want
The dream you put in my heart
It lingers in a deep, dark hole
Waiting to be torn apart
I asked you now a million times
If it's not for me take it away
Don't make me beg for anything
You're not willing to give to me

Maybe I'm doing it all wrong
Maybe I don't understand life
Maybe I'm truly overstrained
And don't know how to do it right

I never get what I truly want
My biggest wish remains unfulfilled
I don't care about anything else
If I can't have this one thing

I surely know that you're in charge
The one who controls everything
But it's hard to understand your plan
Do you even have a plan for me?

People say they see something great
In my future when they look at me
But all I see is a broken, lonely girl
All I see is great debris

And I don't want to go on
I never get what I want
I don't want to go on
I'm not strong enough to hold on
I don't want to go on
Too tired to fake a smile
I never get what I want
My dreams all buried alive

How come I feel so low?
How come I feel this pain?
How come I feel all this sadness?
How come I live my life in vain?

© N. B. 04 / 2016

It's Always Gonna Be OK

I've never really relied on anyone
Everything I went through, I went through alone
I believed that I always had to be strong
But then you came and proved that I was wrong

I had to give up control
Had to let go of it all
You taught me how to trust someone
Something I've never done before
You pulled the carpet from under my feet
While I faced devastation
You showed up in the middle of the darkest scene
While I was consumed by desperation
And you told me
It's gonna be OK
When you're with me
It's always gonna be OK

You have the name above all names
Demons flee when they see your face
Never thought that I could really do that
You brought in color when everything was grey
And I gave it all to you
All my fears and doubts
I gave you all my troubles
All my problems
You carry me through the storm
And you told me
It's gonna be OK
When you're with me
It's always gonna be OK
When you're with me there is nothing I can't face

My Way Is You

I know I make the worst decisions
And make up excuses for everything
I have no idea what's my purpose
At night fear takes over me

There's times when I feel helpless
I close my eyes and say your name
Think about every time you saved me
And trust for you to guide my way

And not one single time
Have you ever let me down
Not one single time have you ever let me down

I know my way is you
My way is through you
My way is you
Only with you

You took me out of this burning hell
With this great yet simple motion
You put your hands on me and cured
This broken soul within seconds

You knew me inside out
Before I walked this cruel, dark world
Even called my name and took me in
When I turned my back on your great love

I was ungrateful
You taught me gratitude
I was unhappy
You gave me fortune
I was ignorant
You taught me how to love
You were my shelter
When I was broken and alone

And not one single time
Have you ever let me down
Not one single time have you ever let me down

I know my way is you
My way is through you
My way is you
Only with you

My Lord, I don't deserve your love

At all

© N. B. 07 / 2015

Love In All The Wrong Places

What is love really?
What is it made of?
What is this feeling?
That makes us soar?
Why do we all pursue it?
What is it we want?
What is love really?
And why does it hurt?

Someone once told me
Love doesn't hurt
It's the absence of love
That causes that harm
A wise woman once said
Love is found everywhere
It is all around us
In every circle and every square

But I was caught in a vicious circle
Running after wrong things
I was trying to force it
But ended up in loneliness
I tried to make love happen
Even though it doesn't work that way
But I guess I somehow believed
That love can be forced to stay

And so love left me
A thousand times
Left my soul to bleed
Emptied my life

I was looking in the wrong places
Hoping for someone to take my heart
Instead they all broke it
And tore it apart

No one would cherish
That they received my trust
No matter what I did
They stepped it into dust

There was only God
Who took my heart as his
And kept it ever so safe
Until the world will perish

In His Embrace

I can't answer your scientific questions
I can't give you quotes to support the facts
Because to me it doesn't really matter
What makes my heart move is different from that
I can't prove any thesis
Cause no matter what I say you'll gainsay me
The only thing I can tell you
Is what happens when he embraces me

I thought no one would ever see me
As I wanted to be seen
I always thought I'm not worth of
Anything good and everlasting
I always thought I can't be forgiven
Of the things I've done and did
The saying that "no one's perfect"
Was comfort enough for me

Never have I thought of being
Holy in any sort of way
It never entered my mind to try it
Cause humans are full of mistakes
I compared myself to others
I'm good to go, never killed anyone
In hell they're looking for true evil
Not for a girl that's simply lost

I can't tell you what has happened to me
I can't really describe what he did
Within a second he changed my whole life
And made me want to become like him
I want to do the things that he did
Tell people there is forgiveness and love
I want the whole world to find him
And experience the miraculous

I can't debate you for your reasons
And I won't fight you on this
Cause the message is so very simple
His love is why we are and why we live
I can only tell you how I feel
When I feel his presence near
How his peace so overwhelms me
And takes away my fears

I wish deep within my inner being
That you'll finally let him in
Cause he's been waiting for you to choose him
Ever since he created you in his image
He loves you more than you imagine
After all he also died for you
If you think that doesn't matter
Let me ask you
Would you ever die for sinners, too?

Angels

The Lord sends forth his angels
They carry you on their arms
They protect you at every chance
Guard you from all possible harm
Cause the Lord said he will rescue you
Because you've come to know his name
And when you call him he will hear you
He'll deliver you from all the pain

You will no longer know despair
The Lord takes it all away
You will no longer know pain
The Lord takes it all away

When you say his name out loud - *Jesus*
He'll take away your doubts
His presence will fill your heart
And make a home within your soul - *Jesus*
Will never leave you alone

While the whole world may be against you
While the whole world may try to change your mind - *Jesus*
Has sent his angels to accompany you
And commanded them to always be by your side

You will no longer know despair; the Lord takes it all away
You will no longer know pain cause the Lord takes it all away

© Natalia Beller 05 / 2017

Lovesick

I cannot describe how I hate this feeling
A lingering feeling of despair
I cannot seem to find a way to
Handle it properly to any extent

I tell myself to stay strong
I tell myself to get through it
I pray for strength to move on
I pray to God to take me in

I really, really detest these experiences
Where I'm left helpless to no end
I really thought that this won't happen again
But then I find myself panting for air

It's so hard for me to breathe
I simply can't understand
I seem to be at the wrong place at all times
Just always a little too late

Lord, I beg for you to take away these feelings
Of jealousy, anger and misery
I beg for you to wash me clean
Take away anything that's not meant for me

You're my only hope to ever be happy
You're the only one that can make me whole
You're the only one I can truly rely on
You're the only one that won't leave me alone

My heart's been broken way too often
One might think I should be accustomed to
Feeling this hurt and this ache inside me
But every time it happens it stings anew

You're the only one I show my pain to
Without covering anything up
For the rest of the world I put on a fake face
A smile to not show the shame that I got

But I don't know how much longer I can go on
At times, I get so tired of this life
To a point where it doesn't make sense
And I don't know why I'm fighting this fight

It takes a very strong soul to live a life for you
Much stronger soul than to live for the devil's cause
But my reward in the end is not with people
It's with you in heaven above the stars

So please Lord, I beg you
Help me to get through this
You have answered every single one of my prayers
Please help me Lord, to get through this

© N. B. 03 / 2016

Inspiration

These words don't come from sadness
Don't come just from joy
They don't come from confessions
They come to me from up above

You're my inspiration
My guidance in the dark
You're my path to liberation
My hope when I'm torn apart

You're my inspiration
The hand that holds me safe and firm
You're my path to liberation
My every single thought

These are the words
You want your children to hear
These are the words
From your heart to theirs

These are the words
You whisper to everyone
"Look up child, there I am
I love you more than you'll ever know"

"For you I died
So, you can live
Yes, I sacrificed
Now, go live for me

I have loved you
Before I formed you in your mother's womb
I have called you
Will you bear your cross and follow the truth?"

These are the words
You want your children to hear
These are the words
From your heart to theirs

These are the words
You whisper to everyone
"Look up child, there I am
I love you more than you'll ever know"

Never Alone

You're always watching
You're always there
Every path I walk, you walk it with me
You always care
And I'm never alone
You're always here with me

You're always listening
My words in your ear
Every thought I have you already know it
You're always near
And I'm never alone
You're always here with me

You hold me back from making mistakes
You remind me of your word
You put on my mind what really matters
You make sure I know your thoughts
And I'm never alone

When everyone leaves me
You're always there for me
You celebrate my victories
Without you there'd be no me

You comfort me in my setbacks
You hold my faith in your palm
You comfort me when I'm upset
You hold me close, keep me calm

You're always with me
And I'm never alone
My comfort in this struggling life is
I have a Father in heaven
Who loves me no matter what

And I'm never alone

© N. B. 05 / 2017

Ladybug

Just hold and kiss me like I'm your first love
Pretend to love me like you never loved someone before
Because my heart's set on you
And you're the only one I want
You're on my mind whatever I do and wherever I go

I want to make this here reality
Sick of seeing you only in my dreams
When I wake up and find myself without you
I'm fighting to go back to sleep

And there's a billion guys in the world
But I only want to be your girl
There's a billion guys in the world
But you're the only one I want

I whisper my love secretly for you to hear
And I think you can replace the missing parts in me
What happened, why am I so drawn to you?
If the world would perish I'd only worry about saving you

And there's a billion guys in the world
But I only want to be your girl
There's a billion guys in the world
But you're the only one I want

Just hold and kiss me like I'm your first love
Pretend to love me like you never loved someone before
Because my heart is set on you
And you're the only one I want
You're on my mind whatever I do and wherever I go

I want to make this here reality
Sick of seeing you only in my dreams
When I wake up and find myself without you
I'm fighting to go back to sleep

Cause there's a billion guys in the world
But I only want to be your girl
There's a billion guys in the world
But you're the only one I want

© N. B. 09 / 2009

Psalms for Jesus

I've been lied to a million times
I've been hurt and disrespected
I shed tears on countless nights
I've been laughed at and neglected

I've heard so many promises
That no one intended to keep
I've seen so much terror
That caused my soul to bleed

You my Lord, know all my struggles
You know every one of my tears
You my Lord, know all of my aching
Have lived every moment with me

And every time I was down
You picked me up again
Every time I was about to give up
You breathed life into me again

I've been left alone and abandoned
When all I wanted was to be loved
I bore much more than necessary
Looking for a shelter from the storm

I believed so many lies
Hoping to find some truth in them
Not knowing that if I only believed in you
I won't ever be disappointed again

Cause every time I was down
You picked me up again
Every time I was about to give up
You breathed life into me again

My life was full of cold frustration
Caused by people that never cared for me
My life turned into a nightmare
Keeping me away from my king

The darkness overwhelmed me
I was scared to turn off the lights
My nights were filled with agony
And hopelessness filled my mind

But one day and out of the blue
There were you
Unimpressed by what I've been through
Unimpressed by what I knew

You were so persistent, so endured
You picked me up among the broken hearted
And made my life anew

© N. B. 02 / 2016

I Don't Want To Live

Others take it as a compliment
The moment you breathed life into them
When amidst of their creation
You designed their destinies and their plans
But I don't see it like that

To me there is nothing worse
Than life itself
This world is cold and so corrupt
And I hate to be there
I don't see a sense in what I do
I don't find joy in anything
To me life is just a punishment
A test we're all failing

There is nothing beautiful
About life and being alive
Others may call this thing a gift
I call it a burden I try to connive
There's not one day that I don't hate
Not one night I wish to finally die
And I can't even go and kill myself
Cause it is forbidden by Jesus Christ

And I pray and pray and pray and pray
For a purpose and a sense
Somehow God gives me the strength
To make it through one more day

But the bottom line remains the same
I really don't want to live
Everything I ever try to do
Is not destined to succeed

A dying dream feels like you're dying, too
So slowly and amidst torment
There's not one single thing to do
And you'll never understand
You will never know what you did wrong
You'll never know the reasons why
You have to take the pain and live with it
Until the day you'll finally die

I really mean the words I say
I really don't want to live
I'm all alone and it feels like hell
Why do I have to go through this?

Every day is exactly the same
There are no ups and no downs
I really, really don't want to live
Please dear God, take me from this world

© N. B. 04 / 2016

Longing For Love

We all know we're loved by our Lord and Savior
In the most abundant way
His blessings never seem to end
Even if we find ourselves going astray
We have a great, great God
And the most wonderful Father
He takes care of everyone each day
Holds us close to not drown in deep waters

We find peace in being with him
His presence means great freedom
We're free from hate and free from fear
And anything that would harm us
Still there are things in this world
That every person needs
Things we dream about and pray for
Like love and intimacy

Humans aren't made to spend their lives alone
To be lonely without a hand to hold
We're not wired to face challenges
Without love that will help us bear it all

We long for someone to wake up to in the morning
Someone next to us when we fall asleep at night
Someone to take us in when we are hurting
Someone to wipe our tears when we cry

And it's ok to cry
It's really ok to cry
The Father will be strong for us

It's ok to cry
It's really ok to break down and cry
The Father is always there to hold us

And one day
When you don't even anticipate
You will stand before someone
That will make you understand

Someone to make sense out of
Someone who'll show you true love
Someone who won't leave you
Cause he'll be sent by God

© N. B. 03 / 2016

Remember Your Dream

This world can make you feel undiscovered
It makes you feel so invisible
This place is huge and makes you feel alone
Like this life is but inconsolable
Though you feel you have so much to offer
You don't even know where to begin
Where should you go to and what should you do then?
You don't know how to describe this conflict

Cause there is this dream inside you
It seems it's always been there
You don't remember exactly how it started
You just remember it's always been there
And even when everything fell apart
This one dream always stuck to you
Even if you found everything shattered on the ground
This dream you have has never ever left you

You don't know how to make it come true
And every day it hurts a little more
You feel like a failure, like you're unworthy
Can't figure out what's this problem's source
In your mind you see it clearly
You see your future before your eyes
You feel it in your heart like true reality
You can smell it when you close your eyes

Just know the Lord was the one that gave you
This dream you can't seem to shake
When he decided to breathe life into you
He gave you all necessary competence
As he said he'll never leave nor forsake you
As he said he'll always stay by your side
This also means you may rest assured
Wherever God leads you he also provides

The Lord is our shepherd, whom shall we fear?
He will also make your dreams come true
Trust in him and know for sure that he'll keep
Every single promise he ever gave to you
Remember your dream when you praise him
Remember your dream when you say thanks
Know deep in your heart that God is in charge
And you forever stay in the palm of God's hand

For every dream there is a perfect timing
According to His timing the Lord will react
Even when you don't see anything changing
God's always working for your best results

Even if you might feel discouraged
Know that the Lord won't give up on you
There is a reason you keep dreaming this dream
It will happen
Because God believes in you

© N. B. 04 / 2016

Evening Prayer

Dear Lord
I want to thank you for this day
I thank you that you're always watching out for me

Dear Lord
I want to thank you for everything
Thank you for catching me when I'm falling

Thank you for my blessings
For every single thing I have in life
If it hasn't been for you
I would have never gotten one thing right
Thank you for my family
Every single person I was blessed to meet
Thank you for every moment
Filled with beautiful memories

Dear Lord
Please go and be so very close
To every person that I know
Touch their hearts
Like you've touched mine
Let them know you
And bless their lives

Dear Lord
In Jesus' name I ask
To help me through the coming days
And walk on the right path

Dear Lord
Help me to fulfill your will
Keep me safe from all temptations
So that I may not sin

Dear Lord
Help me understand your plan
Help me to trust your guidance
Through everything that comes my way

Dear Lord
My life is in your hands
I know what you have in store for me
Is much greater than what I've ever dreamt

Dear Lord
As I say goodnight to you
Guard my sleep and make me sleep tight
Keep me safe
With pleasant dreams
In Jesus name I pray

Amen

© N. B. 07 / 2017

Anniversary

Every day I grow to love you more
It's been over four years now
I can hardly remember
How I lived without you before
Before I gave my life to you
I had trouble to even like myself
Hated the person that I was
Before your voice echoed in my head

Then you called my name
And everything changed

My fears have disappeared
My anxiety was completely healed
You wiped away all of my tears
It's been like this for over four years

I can't imagine to ever live without you
What kind of life would that be?
I can't imagine to ever be without you
What kind of existence would it be?

Since the day you called my name
Everything has changed

And I want the whole wide world to know
How wonderful it is to know you
I want everyone to know
What it's like to live a life with you

I want everyone to experience
What I've experienced with you
I want them to know this peace and comfort
That can only come from you

Because you once called my name
And my entire life has changed

© N. B. 05 / 2017

Yours Not Mine

Why are you so worried?
You have nothing to fear
You're the one that's there with him
Even though he might think of me

It's just thoughts
Nothing serious
I'm not the one he spends his nights with
I'm not the one he wants

He said he liked my name
He liked my eyes
He liked the way I dress
And my smile

But still he goes home with you
With his arm around your waist
I can't change the way I am
And you can't hate me for that

There's no need to check his phone
You won't find my number there
Why are you so paranoid?
Nothing has happened yet
And I promise you nothing ever will
Cause I know who he truly loves
I am just a silent dream
He's been having on and off

He said he liked my laugh
And the way I walk
He said he liked my scent
And the way I talk

But he doesn't even know me
And you know him better than I ever will
Though this might seem threatening
You have nothing to fear

Cause he might want me from time to time
But he's yours and not mine

He is yours not mine

© N. B. 09 / 2009

Mama (You Never Told Me)

Your words will always lay deep within me
The way you taught me everything
The things I learned will always be a part of me
But one thing you have missed

Cause when I lay awake and there's no one to talk to
When I'm alone and this pain inside me grows
When I'm helpless and feel this yearning that won't stop
How come you never told me how to cope?

Mama
Can't you take this hurt away?
When this ache just grows and he's the only one to ever ease this pain
Mama
Why does it have to hurt so bad?
How come you never mentioned, never said
That love can be too much to bear

I never thought that feelings could scare me
That there's one guy who'd be able to hurt me
That I could fall in love with a smile, with *blue eyes*
With things that are so fragile

And when I wish for his arms to be around me
When it's dark and I can't seem to see clearly
When I close my eyes and he's the only thing I need
You never told me about this

And when I saw him walking down the street
His arms wrapped around *her* instead of me
When I felt that my heart would stop beating
You never told me about it

And when I saw his lips touch *hers* instead of mine
And this sting in my chest almost made me die
When I tried to stay strong but broke down inside
You never ever told me how to fight

Mama
When I'm alone and feel it all again
When I try to forget it but it keeps coming back
Why did you never teach me about that?
Mama
When I sleep and dream about him at night
When I hear his voice, and smell his odor one more time
Why did you never tell me that in life
There's this thing called love
Why did you never tell me that it hurts?

Mama
You never told me that it hurts

© N. B. 05/2009 // 07/2017

Isabella

Everything happens for a reason
And now it's been over 21 years
No one knows me like you do
And supports me through everything
You know my worst characteristics
You know me at my best
You know my heart and all my thoughts
Always know the right things to say

You're there for me through it all
Nothing compares to you
There's nothing we can't talk about
Nothing I have to hide from you
I can drop my guard
And tear down all my fences
Because you love me for me
And not for what you may gain

Forever is a word I never believed in
But in your eyes, it all comes true
You know my life and every single story
When I'm down I only want to talk to you

Because I trust you
Like I trust no one else
I can be myself around you
You're the best thing I ever had

Every night I pray to God
He always may protect you
Thank him on my knees
For everything you do
I ask him to shower you with love
So, you don't even hurt your toe
No harm shall come upon you
Only blessings and great hope

You're so patient and understanding
No matter what we face
This right here will go down in history
This isn't just a phase

It's been a whole life
With you by my side
Another life to come
And I won't leave you alone

© N. B. 07 / 2017

The Opposite Of Love

The ache
The pain
The drag
Love in vain
The cold
Truth untold
Wicked words
Made to hurt

Misunderstood
Left for good
Broken dreams
Silent screams
Open eyes
Barely alive
Not to self
Keep your guard
So unexpected
Full of scars

Undeniable
But adorable
Am I unlovable?
It's the opposite of love

Broken down
And in tears
Have never known
Pain like this
What did he do?
Unnecessary
Lied to me, too
I believed his stories

Misunderstood
Left for good
Broken dreams
Silent screams
Open eyes
Barely alive
Not to self
Keep your guard
So unexpected
Full of scars

This is not love
This is the opposite of love

What To Do With A Broken Heart?

What shall I do when I feel worthless?
What to do when I feel left alone?
What to do when I feel like no one cares?
What now, the damage is done

What shall I do when I fall apart?
What to do with a broken heart?

What shall I do when he has moved on?
What to do when no one's there?
What to do when I feel it's too cold?
What shall I do when I've been replaced?

What shall I do when I fall apart?
What to do with a broken heart?

What shall I do when I'm slowly burning?
What to do when there's nothing I can do?
What to do when I'm in so much pain?
That it feels like I can never be cured
What shall I do when I feel misplaced?
What to do when he's all I want?
Where to run to when I feel I'm so lost?
What to do with a broken heart?

What to do when I hate the love that I feel?
What to say when the words won't come out?
What shall I do when I'm insanely hurting?
How to cope with this when I'm broken down?

I feel tired and go to sleep
Place my devastation in front of you
Wake up different in the morning
What has happened, what did you do

Just yesterday I was falling apart
Not knowing what to do with this broken heart
But you're closest to the broken hearted
Close to the ones caught in the dark

And you came to mend my heart
When I was falling apart

God came to mend my broken heart

© N. B. 05 / 2017

Power Of The Cross

Some years ago I found it hard to sleep
I heard dark voices whisper into my ear
I felt gloomy shadows entering my room
Demonic spirits clinging onto my soul
At night I found it hard to rest
Couldn't turn dark thoughts off in my head
I saw figures climbing up my walls
I caved in when the enemy was in control

I couldn't tell anyone about what I was seeing
They might have said I was only dreaming
After all who is able to cure my mind?
I've never even heard of Jesus' sacrifice

I didn't know how to give God my trust
I didn't know that he gave his Son for us
I didn't know that his Son took all the beating
That we deserved for getting deceived

I didn't know that there was hope
No one told me about the power of the cross
I didn't know there's power in Jesus' name
I didn't know demons flee when they see his face

Never knew that I had to turn to him
I didn't know that he forgives my sins
For years I have lived in darkness
Misunderstood, I felt so helpless

I was suffering as everyone suffers, too
It has become quite normal to feel abused
Like a competition who's hurting more
Pain as a standard to define who we are
We're degraded by every problem
Every challenge seems to be another curse
Bound by the enemy to our own weakness
A slave to the evil that rules the world

Only few seem to know that the one inside of us
Is bigger than the one that lives in this world
Only few really put in God their trust
Until our fears almost leave us cold

I wish someone had told me sooner
How to free myself from shame
I wish that I had known a lot sooner
That it only takes Jesus to defeat the pain

When You're With Me

I should feel relieved, safe and warm
I should never doubt anything at all
I should trust you and feel like home
But when you're with me I still feel alone

The things you say don't get me high
The way you kiss does not feel right
The touch of your hand burns my skin
When you're with me I'd rather leave

The sun is shining and still I'm cold
Your arms around me can't warm me up
Your words sound true but I can't listen
When I'm with you there's something missing

I don't feel safe, I've forgotten how it feels
I walked for miles and now I'm dizzy
Thought here would be a place that I belong
But when you're with me it still feels wrong

I don't feel relieved, safe nor warm
I feel like doubting everything I know
I don't trust you, don't feel like home
When you're with me I still feel alone

© N. B. 09 / 2009

Crime Policy

Pick me up and pull me down
Take me and then reject me
Love me and then let me fall apart
Call me and then ignore me

And the siren's ringing loudly
I wish one day you will get caught
You always somehow catch me
And do it from the start

Fill me up and drink me empty
Get me high then detox me
Yell at me then beg for forgiveness
Heal my wounds then cut my wrists

My soul's exposed to you now
And I could never run away
I beg for someone else to help me
But there is no one there

Suck my blood; reanimate me
Call me a whore and then a saint
Tuck me in then quickly wake me
Find a cure then release my pain

You have no manners whatsoever
You have no heart inside your chest
I beg for someone else to help me
But there is no one there

Think of me and then forget me
Rescue me then drown me again
Draw my lines and then erase me
Smile at me then turn right away

My dreams turn into nightmares
Each one of them involving you
I can't scream my voice is fading
Can't bear the pain you put me through

The siren's ringing loudly
I wish one day you will get caught
You always somehow catch me
And do it from the start

My King

You came to me in my darkest hour
You gave me life where there was none
Didn't hesitate to forgive my failures
You came to me when I was all alone
You gave me laughter amidst my tears
You gave me hope in hopelessness
I gave you my hand for you to lead
You held me warm in great coldness
You brought understanding
Into a place of selfishness
You brought peace and healing
Into a place of restlessness
No longer do I have to bear this
You brought in the light
You are the reason I believe
You are the truth, the way and the life
You came to me when no one wanted
You are never leaving me again
You hold your hands up over me
You never let me go astray
You came to bring me comfort
When people were out of words
You came to me when I was broken
You brought joy when I was hurt
You're my Lord and King of all Kings
The only one I will kneel before
You came to me to set me free
Of every shackle that held me down
You took me in when they all left me
You loved me when all I knew was pain
You keep me close in my imperfection
Because of you I'm freed from hate

© N. B. 02 / 2016

She's Sorry

The window's open
And the light's turned on
She stares at the paper
Without reading a word
He said it could be a while
And put his glasses back on
He left the room
And left them alone
She sat there for five days
And there are more to come
She holds his hand
Dreams of the day when his eyes will open up
Tears fill her eyes
As she tucks him in again
The picture's burnt into her mind
She prays for him to come back
His face looks pale
His pulse is steady
He hasn't moved in days
His heart's beating faintly
She's thinking of the day
When he left the house all mad
Why was "*I hate you*" the last thing she said?
And now she regrets
Starts to hate herself
For the pain she caused him and the things she said
Cause she loves him
And she always will
But right now she can't even apologize for what she did
And she's so sorry, oh, what she wouldn't give
Just to look into his eyes and kiss him one more time
And tell him she's sorry

© N. B. 10 / 2009

87

Reconcile

Forgive and you shall be forgiven
Be kind to each other and portray God's love
There is no sin in this world so big
That God will say it's unforgiveable
Nothing you will confess to him
Will ever come to him as a surprise
You might be able to hide from people
But you can't hide anything from the Most High

I know it's hard for you to do
I've been there believe you me
It seems easier to hold on to grudge
Than to accept someone's failing
It seems easier to hold on to the pain
And let the hatred grow
You think you have the right to judge them
And don't see a reason to let it go

But you make yourself a prisoner
Of a past that is long gone
You make yourself a lost slave
Whatever happened is long done
There is only one way
And it's always leading straight ahead
Do not dwell in dark memories
When Jesus died he took them all away

No matter where you stand in your life now
It's never too late to turn to God
He will take you from wherever you are now
And wash you clean by his Son's blood
There is no sin he will not forgive
There is nothing you can do to stop his love
Because he is so infinitely gracious
God is light, there's no darkness in him at all

You are worthy to live freely
You are worthy of the Father's love
You deserve to live out all your dreams
What other's think does not define your worth
Your identity is found in our Savior
Not in the mistakes you made in the past
Not in decisions you think can't be undone
But in our Lord and God, Jesus Christ, alone

Repent and be forgiven
Turn away from your wicked ways
For not by works are we being redeemed
Alone by his Grace we can be saved

© N. B. 03 / 2016

Morning Prayer

Thank you, Father
You're always there for me
You're the only one who always listens
Even when I don't speak
I feel so insanely lucky
That you didn't give up on me
That you called my name
When I was lost
And brought me back where I belong
Thank you, Father
For teaching me
How to live a life for you and not for me
Guided by the Holy Spirit
It's been years
But I still can't believe
That you didn't overlook me
But instead you saved me
So, as I go about this day
See to it that I won't go astray
Guide me through every moment
And send me the right things to say
Show me the right things to do
Point out when I'm in the wrong
Give me strength for every challenge
So that I can make you proud
Help me Lord to project you
When people look at me they shall see you
Help me Lord to speak like you do
To see people not like the world does, but like you do

Whatever circumstance may come my way
You'll be there with me and in Jesus' name I pray, amen

© N. B. 07 / 2017

Love Me In Return

Tell me miracles still exist because I need one
Tell me that if I still believe I will recover
In my worried eyes, you say there's nothing but desperation
In my fragile voice, you say there's nothing but confusion
Tell me miracles still exist so I'll get my own redemption
Tell me that if I just believe I will find salvation
I want to find someone, someone I can trust
Without having to fear they'll burst me into dust
I want to find someone, someone I can love
Without having to fear they won't love me in return
Tell me miracles still exist because I need one
Tell me that if I just believe I will find someone
Someone that will take the pain and replace it all with love
Tell me miracles still exist and I won't abandon hope
I want to find someone, someone I can trust
Without having to fear they'll burst me into dust
I want to find someone, someone I can love
Without having to fear they won't love me in return

Then I found hope in God, I found love in him
I found strength in my faith, I found peace again
I came to see what everyone else was seeing
I came to believe what they were believing
And now I know that miracles still exist, too
I started believing and I was rescued
I was all alone and didn't know how
To hold on anymore
Before I even knew it all pain seemed to be gone
I know I'll find someone, someone I can trust
Without having to fear they'll burst me into dust
I know I'll find someone, someone I can love
Without having to fear they won't love me in return

© N. B. 03/2011 // 07/2017

91

We Are Called To Love

In Jesus Christ, we're all one
There is no difference between you and me
And he called us all to simply love
No matter what someone said or did
It has become so seldom
We're taught love is ought to be earned
But it's a gift straight from God
We can love because He first loved us

We're called to go out to all nations
And proclaim His sacrifice
Tell the world there is redemption
Tell the world He paid the price
We're called to spread the Gospel
Tell the whole world the Good News
That God is alive and that He saved us
Took the punishment that we deserved

We're not the ones to judge one another
We are simply called to love
We're not allowed to pronounce a sentence
We are simply called to love

This generation became so proud
They can't even say it out loud
We're simply called to love
Not in moderation but a lot

So if you can't forgive your neighbor
If you feel you can't forgive anyone
Reflect yourself and don't lose sight of
All the things that you've done wrong
You're not perfect either
No one walking this earth truly is
There is more to us than meets the eye
More sin in us than we're willing to admit

Always remember the things that you did
Remember that God forgave you, too
Everyone deserves to be forgiven
No matter how bad you think they treated you
Your cup is just as full as theirs is
You're not more holy than anyone else
Remember we're called to live in love
Nothing is greater than God and his Grace

We're not the ones to judge one another
We are simply called to love
We're not allowed to pronounce a sentence
We are simply called to love

This generation became so proud
They can't even say it out loud
We're simply called to love
Not in moderation but a lot

© N. B. 05 / 2016

Blue Moon

If you intend to hurt me
You're doing very well
If you intend to make me bleed
I'm under your spell
Not able to move or run away
You can just keep on going this way
Doesn't seem like I mind the pain
Anyway

Cause I know I'll get through this
Somehow, I'll get through this again
God will never leave me
He will mend my heart and ease the pain
There's no need to feel sorry for me
I don't need anyone's help in this
God will come and help me out
Like he's done a thousand times before
I can't find the words to tell you
What I'm keeping safe in mind
If we were meant to be you would know
And I wouldn't have to hide

So I don't think I need to tell you
The things I keep in mind
Cause you won't see what I mean
And I'd still lose sleep on this at night
Long ago I've been told
Only once in a blue moon
Does a heart find its other half
And my other half can't be you

It can't be you

© N. B. 07 / 2017

Forever

This right here is not my home
This life I live is temporary
Forever is something so much more
A life that comes right after this
We all have to make a choice for the life of forever
And which choice will you make, for the life of forever

Jesus provided the sacrifice
He paid the full price
You were bought back from the darkness
The moment that he died
The Lamb took away
All sin from this world
By his wounds we were healed
By the pouring of his blood
You have no guarantee of living till you're eighty-six
Your life can end in an instant
Are you prepared for what comes after this?
Cause you have this time right now
A short time compared to forever
This right here is not even your home
Are you ready for forever?

The Most High is in hot pursuit of you
You keep ignoring his voice
Since your birth he's been watching over you
There's nothing he doesn't know
He knows your heart, he knows your name
He loved you before you were born
He knows every word you've ever said
We all have to make a choice for the life of forever
And which choice will you make, for the life of forever

© N. B. 05 / 2017

95

Died Too Young

It's been twelve years
I can't believe it
I will never forget the moment I heard about it
The phone rang
And I heard her voice saying
Andreas is dead
I, too felt like dying

You were taken away from me
Away from this world
You were taken away
Way too young
Why did it have to happen?
God, why didn't you protect him?
Just two seconds, two simple seconds
And he'd still be here with me

And I blame myself
No one knows about this
That day you've been on my mind the whole time
And I felt too lazy to get up and react to it
You've been on my mind
I blame myself for your dying
If I only had the nerve to do what God told me to do
I wouldn't stand here crying

Now you're gone
You won't return
I see your face when I close my eyes
Remember the day
March 8th, you came
"Natalia, I have a surprise"

Five months later
No more you
Won't hear your voice again
Why did the Lord
Take the best of them all
I'd sell my soul to see you again

I keep picturing all the things we could have experienced
If only we had more time
No one is like you and you can never be replaced
You'll forever be a part of my life
When I leave this world and it's my turn for farewell one day
I know in heaven I'll see your smile
All of this won't matter anymore, we'll be together again
But for now, I break down and cry

Cause I miss you
Oh God, how I miss you
You were the best thing in this lifetime

Dear Lord

Dear Lord, I don't want to doubt you
But I'm really starting to doubt
How many times will I have to suffer?
When will this aching stop?

What have I done to deserve this?
What is this thing I'm punished for?
Lord, why do I have to bear this?
Why is there so much hurt?

Life's not beautiful, it's simply unfair
Blessings are shared unjust
The righteous ones bear sickness
While the wicked ones bathe in luck

I can't take this inequity
I don't understand your plans at all
I wish that maybe just a little bit
Misfortune is shared identical

Dear Lord, you hear my prayer
I know you always hear my plea
Why, oh Lord, don't I see any changes?
Why does this misery never leave?

Oh, when will your blessing come upon me?
When will it be my turn to shine?
Dear Lord, when will you finally reveal?
Concerning me, what's on your mind?

Dear Lord, you know all of my heartache
You know how much I want to love
You know about my deepest wishes
And what I'm truly longing for

So, how long will you keep me waiting?
Cause I can't take this anymore
My life I've given to you completely
But I'm terrified of dying alone

© N. B. 02 / 2016

Don't Make Them Feel The Same

I admit it, I feel envy
Whenever I see another happy face
People living life so easily
Away from sadness and from hate
I wonder what it feels like
To have everything you dreamt of
I wonder what it feels like
To never be alone

Then I remember the pain that I feel
Realize the ache and hurt inside my heart
Caused by undisclosed desires
Silently buried dreams torn apart
And I quietly ask the Lord
To never make anyone else feel this way
Don't want anyone else to be this miserable
Don't want anyone else to feel the same

I've been feeling this for a long, long time
I am so very used to this
I ask the Lord our God not to pass it on
Give them all the things they need
I will not simply break down and cry
Though I feel like I'm on the verge of it
I'm strong enough to take this every time
I will make it through all of it

No matter how hard it gets
I'll never give into dark thoughts
But everyone else might get lost
No matter how tough it gets
I'll never give into dark thoughts
But the others may not be that strong

So, I ask you Lord, don't make them feel this
Don't let anyone else feel this depressed
Take their hearts fill them with happiness
Don't let them drown in their distress

Take each and every single soul
Even the ones that don't know your name
Give them hope and uplift their faith
So, they will never feel this way

Don't let them feel the same

© N. B. 04 / 2016

Falling In Love

This got me asking
What is wrong with me?
What is it that I do?
Is it that I exude something?
Is there something repellent?
About whom I'm trying to be
Who am I at all?
I've never felt so self-deceived

They say I should pray more and worry less
But I can't even find the words
They say I should throw my burdens all on you
But I don't know how to let it go
It's not that I doubt you're able
To take care of everything
I just never learned to let go
Of things that tend to hurt me

Lord, my God
Why do you allow me to have these feelings?
Lord, my God
I cannot handle them at all
I don't know how to hold on
I have no clue how to even go on

I find it so hard to breathe
Because I know he's fine without me
Lord, my God
Please come and save me from this

You are always my refuge
My shelter from the storm
You always keep me sane
When insanity overflows
But now I can't think clearly
I see his face when I close my eyes
Please take away all these loving feelings
For a man that will never be mine

God is Love
Love's supposed to be good
Our God is light
In him there is no darkness at all
But now I feel like falling into darkness
By falling in love with him
And I don't understand why
What did I do to deserve all this?

© N. B. 03 / 2016

So Real

Everytime I feel down
I just close my eyes
Listen to the sound of your voice
And imagine a different life
Feel like I'm holding it in my hands
It feels like I'm standing right here
I can smell the difference
And feel the fear disappear

I absorb this feeling
Memorize the joy
The way it feels I can't be dreaming
The truth is in your voice
I feel a smile conquering my lips
Feel your warm embrace
It feels so real, just like I imagined
Just a stone's throw away

I feel the sun warming my skin
Even though it's raining now
And the frustration's being buried
Deep beneath the ground
Everytime I feel down
I just close my eyes
Listen to what your voice says
And I imagine a different life

And I know that one day
When I close my eyes again
I will open them without being scared
I won't be asleep I'll be awake
Cause I know that one day
This dream will be reality
And I won't have to close my eyes again
To imagine it is here

So real that I can feel it
So real that it makes me cry
So real that I can touch it
So real that I'll start to cry

© N. B. 07 / 2017

Far Better Than Me

I wish I could look like her
Those lips and perfect skin
I wish I could sound like her
She thinks before she speaks

I wish I was that beautiful
As wonderful and unique
I wish I could look like her
Her appearance is majestic

I wish I could be like her
Such congeniality
I wish I could be like her
Perfect smile and vibrancy

I wish I could be like her
Her hair falls perfectly
Her long legs and perfect hands
I wish I looked like that

I wish I could be this way
And have the things she has
I wish I could have her ways
And make you simply melt

I wish I'd have what it takes
To steal your heart away
I wish I'd have the things she has
That made you turn your head

I wish I could be like her
Such charisma is unique
I wish I could be like her
And you'd fall in love with me

I wish I could look like that
And be the one you truly see
I wish I knew how to act like her
I wish you'd care for me

I wish I'd have what it takes
To make you fall for me
I wish I'd have that pretty face
Silky hair and pouty lips
I wish I'd have that rosy scent
To make you notice me

But I'm not her
I can't be her
She's far better than me

© N. B. 01 / 2011

A Love I will Never Have

Dear God I know you hear me
I know that every word I think you know it
Before I begin to speak
Dear God you know how I'm feeling
You know what I'm going through before I
Understand myself

So now explain to me
This misery
Tell me how to deal with it
So much I want to do
But it feels like I'm tied up
Though I really want to fight
I can't seem to step out at the right time

And I'm helpless
So confused
I'm not used to feeling this exhausted
I feel shattered
And abused
By my own decisions and thoughts

Dear God please give me an answer
I have so many questions in my head that
I can't seem to shake
Dear God please cure this awful cancer
How much longer will this go on like that

Please reveal to me your remedy
I cannot cope alone with this
Why does this feel like slowly dying
I know I'm alive but I don't feel like it

© N. B. 07 / 2017

Simone

Your heart is unique
All the words that you speak
No one is this understanding
No one is that supportive
The way you feel for everyone
Compassion in your heart
The way you're able to comfort
Is so one in a million

Like an oak you're standing strong
Though you've faced the worst of all possible fates
Like an angel with a bright halo
You're bringing joy to everyone crossing your path

Your smile lights up all rooms
Your touch is caring and so smooth
Your eyes reflect your soul
Nothing dark inside you at all

I love the way you are
So pure and uncomplicated
So emotional, you're my star
So true and advocated
Lord I thank you for having her
I ask you to shield all harm from her
Bless her in abundant ways
Shower her with your amazing grace

Like a breeze that's softly blowing
Like a ray of light piercing through the clouds
Like a rose grown so beautifully
You're there for me to take away all doubts

I love you more than you know
To you I dedicate these thoughts
Like a pencil gliding on a piece of paper
It comes to me so natural

Stay the way you are
Cause to me you're perfect
Stay the way you are
You make each moment perfect

© N. B. 07 / 2017

Reality

What have you done?
Why are you doing this to me?
Where have I gone?
Why do I suffer like this?
It's highs and lows
It's tears and sorrow
I go to sleep feeling OK
But wake up filled with horror

I can't describe this situation
Only God knows what's going on
I can't escape this deep depression
Lord, please help me to move on

Cause the one I love
He loves another
The one I want
Wants someone else
All I dream about
Is being with him
All I truly want
Is to be his own

But the one I love
Does not love me in return

I can't stop picturing us together
I can't stop caring just because he doesn't care
How do I get rid of all these feelings?
How to erase every moment we ever shared?

Lord, this is when I need you most
Lift me up and heal my wounds
My heart is bleeding
My soul is screaming
This ache seems to be choking me
It's so hard to breathe

The one I adore
Adores another
The one I think about
Never thinks of me
All I desire
Is to have him with me
I'd die for him
He doesn't care for me

Why do I need him?
Cause I know I need him
Why do I need him?
So badly

The one I love
Does not love me in return

© N. B. 07 / 2017

Spoken Words Still Unspoken

I have so much to tell you
But when you look at me
I become so numb
I have so many things to show you
But when I see your eyes
I feel so stunned

Something about you
Something no one else has
Something that God has put in you
For us to meet, was it God's plan?

Something about you
I can't help but loving you
With all my heart and all my soul
Did God intent for me to fall for you?

It seemed like fate
The odds of us meeting where so slight
It seems you are everything
I've been looking for all my life

Why is this so hard?
Why can't we escape and leave the world behind?
Why does it tear me apart?
Ain't love supposed to heal you and lift you high?

But here I stand
Alone, without you
Here I am
Dreaming about you

You're far away
I don't even know what you're doing
You could be anywhere
With anyone
I wonder if you're thinking about me

Something about you
Something no one else has
Something that God has put in you
For us to meet, was it God's plan?

Something about you
I can't help but loving you
With all my heart and all my soul
Did God intent for me to fall for you?

© N. B. 07 / 2017

<u>You, Instead of Him</u>

When I met him
You were on my mind
When he called me
I thought about you all the time
When he took me out
It was you I thought about
When he spoke to me
I thought of you instead of him

He gave me red roses
I wished they were from you
He called me cute nicknames
I was still haunted by you
He drove me home, kissed me good night
I wished for your lips to be touching mine
And when he looked deep into my eyes
I thought of you every single time

It's you instead of him
It's you I truly want
It's you, not really him
You're the one I want

When he asked me how I felt
I couldn't shake the thought of you again
When he touched my hand and pulled me close
I had to step back, didn't want to hurt him more
Because he's not the one I want

I can't help it
I don't know what you did
I always think of you

I'd rather die alone
Than ever be with someone
Someone that isn't you

He did all the right things
But he isn't you

He said all the right things
But he still isn't you

He could be absolutely perfect
I'd still only want you

I love your eyes, I love your smile
I only love you

© N. B. 07 / 2017

<u>I Fear He Will Never Know</u>

Sometimes I have this urge
To stand in front of you
And scream how I feel into your face
Cause I cannot take the hurt
To always be without you
And keep feeling so damn helpless

Is this what my life has now become?
Before I met you, I was fine
I curse the day when I first saw you
I thought it would be different this one time

Lord I love you
But why do you allow for me to feel this pain?
Lord I beg you
Take away the confusion and this ache

I cannot shine anymore
He stole my light
I cannot smile anymore
I'm dead inside

I'm numb to every feeling of bliss
Every moment of happiness
He makes me feel so miserable
Lord I beg you, take care of this

Please

And it's these days I hate the most
I simply don't know what to do
My heart wants him to be close
And I fear he'll never know

I fear he'll never know
How I love him so

I can never let him know

© N. B. 07 / 2017

The Greatest Challenge

Once again, I find myself
Lost in thoughts about this crazy mess
Once again, I start dreaming
Relive your moves over again

I dust off the past
I made it through it
It made me stronger
God helped me get through it
Lessons I've learned
Swore to not repeat mistakes
Learned to forgive
Learned to forget all the pain

But here I am again
Facing the greatest challenge

Cause I'm in love
And I want to tell him
I think I'm in love
How can I tell him?
Does he see me?
Like I see him?
Does he feel for me?
The way I feel for him?

What if the answer is yes?
But it doesn't work out?
How am I going to handle?
Another broken heart
What if the answer is yes?
But he finds I'm not good enough?
Will I be able to handle?
The day when he leaves me alone?

And here I am again
Facing the greatest challenge

The heart is deceitful above all things
What am I supposed to do?
I hate feeling so helpless
He seems too *perfect* to be true

And here I am again
Facing the greatest challenge

Cause I'm in love
But how could I ever tell him?

© N. B. 06 / 2017

Unfair

It's simply unfair
To want someone so much
And not be able to do anything about it
God, I love him so much

It's simply unfair
To have all these feelings inside
And not be able to tell him just a little bit
Instead I always have to hide

I have to respect his decision
His feelings for someone else
Besides he doesn't give me attention
Obviously, he doesn't care
And it's simply unfair

Why this unrequited love?
Why this heartache?
My friends do their best to comfort me
Why this unrequited love?
Can't get him out of my head
I don't understand why this happened to me

I have to go on and live my life
And make peace with the fact he's not mine
As unfair as this might seem to me
There is nothing I can do to change anything

I have to understand this wasn't meant for me
Convince myself there's a reason for all of this
But see, I never fall in love this easily
Something about him makes me crazy

Though I don't really know what it is

It's simply unfair
To want someone so much
And not be able to do anything about it
God, I love him so much

But I have to respect his decision
His feelings for someone else
Besides he doesn't give me attention
Obviously, he doesn't care
And it's simply unfair

It's simply unfair
To have all these feelings inside
And not be able to tell him just a little bit
Instead I always have to hide

© N. B. 07 / 2017

Jennifer

I was heartbroken by the news
I was on the verge to cry
I felt like my whole life was over
All because of one single guy

She saw my sadness
And amidst my tears she came to me
She poured out her love
And then she said to me

"Girl, you're beautiful
So intelligent
You're incomparable
One in a million

Be your own best friend
He doesn't see your true worth
Don't cry over his nonexistent feelings
Don't bring yourself down

You will get through this
There is a reason why we met
There is a reason for everything
This you should never forget

Girl, you're so beautiful
One of a kind without a doubt
Any guy should feel lucky
To ever call you his own

So don't drown in sadness
Wipe away your tears
Remember your faith
Remember why God has put you here

Girl, I love you
Maybe this won't mean a thing
But remember all these words
One day you'll understand all of this"

I drove myself home
Thinking she was right
Still couldn't hold back the tears
But they felt lighter this time

Now everytime I feel a little sad
I remember her words
God sent me an angel
To hold me through the storm

© N. B. 07 / 2017

Woman After Gods Own Heart

No one expects you to be perfect
And never make any mistakes
Lower your expectations towards yourself
You'll sometimes still to go astray
But as long as you'll find your way back
To the Father high above the clouds
You don't have to be perfect
For him to call you his own

You don't have to know every answer
To every question shown
You don't have to be the strong one
That carries the burdens all alone
You don't have to hide your cried tears
You don't have to conceal the way you feel
You don't have to bite your lips
When all you want to do is scream

Cause the Father in heaven knows you
And you've always put him first
You love him with all your soul
And proudly keep his word
But you don't have to be perfect
To be a woman after His own heart
You've done all the right things
For him to know who you truly are

You don't have to prove yourself to others
It's impossible to please every pair of eyes
The only one that truly matters
Is our Lord and Savior, the Most High
And he knows your whole life story
He knows everything and even more
As long as you have his approval
You're a woman after God's own heart

Who Am I?

Sometimes when your Spirit overcomes me
Overflows in this room
I can't manage to hold back my tears
I'm held by the deepest of all loves
Never thought I could love someone
I've never seen face to face
But you're more real than anything in this world
You're closer than anyone else

But who am I to deserve this undying love?
Who am I?
The daughter of the Most High

Who am I?
The daughter of the Most High
Who am I to deserve this sacrifice?

When I think back on what I've done
I feel ashamed by the things I did wrong
All those times I've offended you
All times I rejected you and your word
When I lay awake and it's all quiet
Not a single sound to be heard
I hear you whisper silently into my ear
„I love you daughter, you make me so proud"

But who am I to deserve this love declaration?
Who am I?
The daughter of the Most High

Who am I?
The daughter of the Most High
Who am I to deserve this Grace upon my life?

Every morning that I wake
You're the first thing on my mind
The times I've tried to find love in the wrong places
Are now very far behind

I learned to only depend on you
I learned to trust you with everything
And most times I can't even comprehend
All those amazing things you've done for me

Who am I to deserve this exceptional father?
Who am I?
The daughter of the Most High

Who am I?
The daughter of the Most High
I found my identity in your eyes

© N. B. 05 / 2017

I Hope That You Remember Me

For whatever happened
It happened
No one is truly to blame
Maybe it's my fault
Maybe it's yours
But whatever happened it happened
You'll always have a place in my heart

You are special
And I want you to never forget
I've met many people in this life
Very few this memorable
As I move on
Keeping your face in my memory
I hope that as you move on
You'll sometimes remember me

Maybe when you wake up
Maybe sometime during the day
Maybe when you see something that makes you smile
Maybe in the middle of the night when you lay awake

If our paths never cross again
I want you to know how much joy you've given me
Maybe one day, if it's God's will, we'll meet again
And I can tell you how I feel

The wrong place, the wrong time
Your heart's set on someone else
I'm trying to keep fighting this fight
But this situation I can't change

Cause I can't sleep
I can't eat
I can't get you out of my mind
I can't focus
I can't function
Can't get you out of my mind

You're so damn special
And I want you to never forget
I've met many people in this life
Very few this memorable
As I move on
Keeping your face in my memory
I hope that as you move on
You'll sometimes remember me

I hope that you remember me

© N. B. 07 / 2017

I'm Sorry

Lord, I'm sorry
I hurt someone
I think I made a mistake
And he felt he was lead on
Lord, forgive me
The damage is done
I played his heart like a game
And I am fully at fault

I didn't know what I was causing
I had no idea he cared so much
He does not want my apologies
I think he kind of hates me now

And I deserve it
I really deserve it
I broke his heart

Lord, I'm sorry
What have I done?
Why didn't I tell him honestly?
That I actually want another one

Lord, can you forgive me?
How did I let this happen?
I was selfish, I was evil
I didn't even feel like myself

I never meant for his heart to break
I never wanted to go this far
I thought I had it all under control
But I lost track and tore him apart

And I hear the whispers in the night
"What have you done?"
I hear the whispers in the night
"You evil one"

Lord, forgive me
I can't live with this guilt
Forgive me
Do I deserve it?
I think I deserve it

And I'm so sorry

© N. B. 07 / 2017

Why Couldn't It Have Been Me?

Why am I so aware of my own breathing?
It gets harder every day
Every moment feels like an eternity
I can't forget his face
Will I ever see you again?
Without being too obvious
Will there ever be a chance for us?
For my drama, I'm quite notorious

And I'm so sick of thinking of you
Oh God, take these thoughts away
I'm so fed up with missing you
Oh God, please take these feelings away
And make me whole again

Lord make me the one I was
Before I ever saw his face
Before I ever heard his voice
Before I was doomed to stay in this place

Lord give back my happiness
And my will to live
Cause living life without him here
Is too much to bear for me

Just to think that when I'm here
And he's far away
He's far away with someone else
Just to know that when I think of him
And my thoughts replay
He's thinking about someone else

I hate this
I hate everything about it
I hate every moment of every single day
Why is fate unjustly?
I can't make my peace with this
Why wasn't I the one he saw that day?

Why couldn't it have been me?
Why wasn't it me?
Oh Lord, please tell me why?
Why wasn't it me?

Why couldn't it have been me?

Does She Even Know?

I can't help but wonder
Does she even know?
Does she know how lucky she is?
I would like to ask her
Now that she has the one I love
Does she understand how lucky she is?

She has the most *perfect* man
I have ever met
Does she take him for granted?
She has the most *amazing* man
That I have ever met
Does she appreciate him?

Does she make him breakfast every morning?
And send him cute messages?
Does she wake up next to him smiling?
And kiss him good night when she goes to bed?

Does she do the things I want to do?
Does she take care of him like I would?
Does she know how much he's worth?
Or is she blind to what he deserves?

Does she call him to make sure he's alright?
Dream about him like I do all the time?
Does she know how to make him happy?
Or is she always being selfish?

Does she understand that there is someone like me?
Who'd do anything to have him right beside me?
Does she fulfill all his desires and dreams?
Does she know how damn lucky she is?

She has the most *perfect* man
Does she even know this?
She has the most *amazing* man
Does she appreciate it?
I don't think she does
And I don't think she knows
Because no one has so much love for him
Like I do right now

I'd clean the path for him that he walks on
I'd always be there for him when he'd call
I'd give him everything and only the best
I'd get his name tattooed across my chest

Now let's be honest
Without shame
Would she do the same?

© N. B. 07 / 2017

You Made A Fool Of Me

I think back of the times
I set the world in motion
Just to see you once again
How could I've been so stupid?
Controlled by emotions
Just to maybe have a chance

I can't believe the things I did
Can't believe all the efforts
I've never done anything like this
I feel like a perfect loser

Not one single trace of attention
Have you tossed my way
Didn't look at me once
Felt like you were running away

You really made a fool of me

I thought I could make you fall for me
And now I really hate myself
You don't care and you never will
Just keep on running away

Cause you made a fool of me

And I'm not mad at you
I'm mad at myself
Why was I such a fool?
What happened to me?

It's true, love causes oddness
The strangest behaviors even in adults
Our hearts and minds in a battle
A war we're waging with no result
And I let you make a fool of me
Instead of just stepping back
I can't believe that I ever believed
We could be a perfect match

I don't know what it was
I had this little bit of hope
That if only you would know
We could become so much more

But you chose
To make a fool of me
You rather chose
To go and refuse me

You didn't hesitate to make a great fool of me

© N. B. 07 / 2017

In The Winter

When the rays of the sun warm me up
I feel no fear
I fear no evil
But when I think about what is yet to come
I feel dreaded
Yes, I get scared

Cause the cold of the winter months
It will be another sad time for me
Short days and such long nights
Won't be able to create memories

I'll hide underneath my blanket
Write short stories and some poems, too
Think about how I miss the summer
And I will drown in thoughts of you

I will wish for you to be beside me
I will long for the touch of your hand
I will fantasize about having dinner with you
And watch a movie with you right there

I will imagine what it would feel like
To tell you jokes until you're out of breath
I will desire to have your arms around me
While I'm outside smoking a cigarette

I will wish to cuddle up next to you
And listen to you speak
I'll want to kiss you and tell you I love you
And you'll say the same to me

We will reminisce and laugh together
See how my thoughts have me so obsessed?
But you won't be there, I'll be all alone
What could I possibly do to make you care?

That's why I fear the winter
All my prayers circle around it
Lord spare me that time of the year
I don't want to relive it

In my mind, I made a home with you
It's warm and cozy and where I'd want to stay
The winter time will only remind me
I am here but you're so far away

So, while the rays of the sun warm me up
I'll be happy
I will smile
I try not to think about what is yet to come
Cause it scares me
I want to run away

© N. B. 07 / 2017

It's OK

It's OK
I'll survive
I need to make up my mind
It's really OK
I won't die
I think I can make up my mind

Acceptance of what you don't want
Is never easy
Living with the dreadful memory
That it didn't work out
The heart wants what it wants
And the mind boggles
But reality remains the same
As well as all thoughts

But I think it's OK
Because there's nothing I can do anyway
I can't force you to love me
I can't make you feel the same
That's why it's alright
I'll have to move on with my life
Focus on myself and be fine
Erase all pictures from my mind

Like a sunken ship there's no turning back
Like a fixed broken plate that still has cracks
Like the reflection of my eyes full of pain
I will have to accept my love was all in vain
And I think it's OK

It would have been way too good to be true
Lord knows I never wanted anything more
It would have been heaven down on earth
But you don't seem to love me in return

And I'm sure I'll survive
Somehow, I will make it
Someday I will wake up and smile about it
Won't remember a single thing

One day I will look back on this
And not understand what I did
Cause one day I'll be so OK
That I'll find sense in all of this

Is This Goodbye?

Is this all there is?
Is there more to come?
This thing with you and me
How will it go on?
Is this really goodbye?
We didn't even start
Is this all there is?
It breaks my heart

Jesus, don't take this away from me
Don't let this one end like the ones before
Please, oh Lord, have mercy on me
I've never wanted someone so much before

What can I do?
What can I say?
Where can I go?
To see him again?
What choice do I have?
He's so far away
Won't respond to my plea
I'm stuck in the pain

Jesus, please help me it can't end like this
You're the only one that could do something
Please, oh Lord, don't let me break from it
You're the only one to achieve anything

Where's my comfort?
I'm crying here
Is this now over?
Don't want to believe
Can't erase the thoughts
I'm so naïve
Cause I love him so
Why can't we be?

Jesus, please tell me is this all there is?
You know my heart, my love is sincere
Please, oh Lord, don't you abandon me
You're the only one to make this real

It doesn't enter my mind
This can't be goodbye
I can't say that I'm fine
If this is goodbye
I'm really not fine

Is this goodbye?

© N. B. 07 / 2017

Outro

For over 2 ½ years I have been writing these poems and have been collecting and reliving memories to give someone else out there hope and encouragement. Everytime I was down or sad I needed an outlet for all emotions to be able to start the healing process. For this book, I have written over 200 poems, but I felt that God wanted me to pick 77 in order to create it. In many prayers, I have asked God why he has given me the gift of writing and what he wants me to do with it. The answer was simple: "Serve others". And here I am now, serving _you_. Nothing I have gone through was in vain, if it was able to help at least one person. I was 12 years old when I wrote my first lyric. Back then I had no idea where this journey would take me. Now, today, here I am sharing my deepest emotions with you. I have loved sharing these with you and I hope I get to share even more with you in the future.

So, I want to thank you for reading this. Thank you for taking time out of your life to drown into my thoughts and memories.

Be blessed, always.

Never forget, God loves you.

More than you know...

Instagram: miss_bababelle
Facebook: facebook.com/missnataliabeller